Dear Michelle,

You are so easy to hug!
So grateful to have you as
a good friend! Love you

Happy birthday
2014!
...
Patricia H

THE 10
ESSENTIAL
Hugs
OF LIFE

PRAISE

"When Roy Spence starts talking, I start listening. Next, I ordinarily start nodding my head in agreement. Then, I begin beaming or tearing up (sometimes both at the same time!). Finally, my heart just swells with pride. Why? Because Roy possesses such rare emotional intelligence that he instinctively and intuitively understands that intangibles are more important than tangibles, especially when it comes to matters of the heart. Roy has many accomplishments and accolades on his bio; but I think this enjoyable book is his highest achievement thus far because he is sharing his soul with us. In short, I suspect all readers of this book will walk away from it with a renewed faith in people and in all matters pertaining to the heart."

—Colleen Barrett, president emeritus, Southwest Airlines Co.

"I love this book! I have always believed in the power of the hug. It has been my sole intention these last sixteen years to be sure that as many kids as possible learn that power–and 120 million teddy bear hugs later, I believe we have influenced a generation of girls and boys that it is more than OK to HUG! One thing I know for sure, a HUG is understood in any language. *The 10 Essential Hugs of Life* is a simple reminder that the world is far more bearable when we follow the lessons of HUGS. Thank you, Roy and Jared, for helping us show the world that a HUG is worth a thousand words!" —Maxine Clark, founder, Build-A-Bear Workshop®

"Roy does it. I do it. People like John Mackey and Walter Robb of Whole Foods Market do it. Bert Jacobs of Life is Good does it. We talk about the power of love in business at every stop. My friend Roy Spence teaches us that just as the act of hugging speeds up the process of building a lasting friendship, it also speeds up the process of building lasting business relationships—with employees, vendors, and customers. The world and the world of business are better places because Roy is out there proving through "high-love, high-profit organizations" that hugs are not only OK in virtually any situation, but that they are essential to a happy, loving, fulfilling, and purposeful life and business."

—Kip Tindell, chairman and CEO, The Container Store

"Wow—I thought I understood the value of a hug until I read Roy's wise and delightful book. It will wrap its arms around you and lift you up! And whether you love hugs or avoid them, you owe it to yourself (and your loved ones) to be embraced by this book. *The 10 Essential Hugs of Life* will open your eyes and heart to one of the true wonders of being human: the ability to connect deeply through simple expressions of care. This book is the eleventh hug!"

—Doug Rauch, former president, Trader Joe's Company

"When Roy speaks, I listen. I love how he reminds us once again that love, care, and hugs are essential to leadership, companionship, and being human."   —Walter Robb, co-CEO, Whole Foods Market

THE 10
ESSENTIAL
Hugs
OF LIFE

ROY SPENCE

ILLUSTRATIONS BY JARED DUNTEN

GREENLEAF
BOOK GROUP PRESS

Published by Greenleaf Book Group Press
Austin, Texas
www.gbgpress.com

Publisher's Cataloging-In-Publication Data
(Prepared by The Donohue Group, Inc.)

Spence, Roy.
The 10 essential hugs of life / Roy Spence ; illustrations by Jared Dunten. —1st ed.

p. : ill. ; cm.

Issued also as an ebook.
ISBN: 978-1-62634-026-8

1. Hugging. 2. Spence, Roy. 3. Conduct of life. I. Dunten,
Jared. II. Title. III. Title: Ten essential hugs of life

BF637.H83 S646 2013
158.2   2013941744

Illustrations by Jared Dunten. Jared is a member of
Mouth and Foot Painting Artists, www.mfpausa.com.
To view more of Jared's work and order prints of the illustrations, go to www.jdunten.com.

On the cover and chapter openers: Hugs was lettered by Austin calligrapher and
artist, Liz Hamel. You can view more of Liz's work at www.lizhamel.com.

Distributed by Greenleaf Book Group LLC

For ordering information or special discounts for bulk purchases, please contact
Greenleaf Book Group LLC at PO Box 91869, Austin, TX 78709, 512.891.6100.

Part of the Tree Neutral® program, which offsets the number of trees consumed in
the production and printing of this book by taking proactive steps, such as planting
trees in direct proportion to the number of trees used: www.treeneutral.com.

TreeNeutral®

13 14 15 16 17 18 10 9 8 7 6 5 4 3 2 1
First Edition

CONTENTS

"Every day you should reach out and touch someone. People love a warm hug, or just a friendly pat on the back."

—Maya Angelou

THE STORY OF HUGS

Hugs lift people up, heal hurts,
and spread love.

Genuine hugs give people freedom to be audaciously caring. They are an act of pure human love, and they give people new ways to build bridges, heal hurts, and put a little more joy in the lives of those we touch. No one should go hugless. Hugs are free. And best of all: when you hug, you get hugged back.

I come from a family of huggers. Especially my dad, Roy Milam Spence, Sr., or "Big R," as many people called him. He was born in the culturally rich, economically poor border town of Eagle Pass, Texas, in 1913. His mother passed away when he was young. Like all pre-Depression kids, he and his sister and two brothers pretty much lived hand to mouth. His daddy, Roy Moore Spence, did all he could, but those were the times. His values of family, hard work, love of our nation, and cherishing the good in the world were forged in an age defined by challenge and loss, but also by the power of community. He was tested under fire as a teenager, and the fire lost. He grew up in the epicenter of the Great Depression, but he was never depressed. He had to drop out of school when he was young to support his family, but he never dropped out of life.

Dad married my mom, Ruth Spence—the best mom and the best schoolteacher in the world—in 1941. He then joined the Navy during World War II, and my mom moved to Brownwood, Texas, to live with my grandmother and granddad. That is where she and my dad settled when he returned from the war. Along with my most excellent sisters, Susan and Mary Gordon, I was lucky to have an awesome childhood in that little town, a childhood full of friends, love, security, encouragement, and yes, hugs.

Dad and I had many great and frankly remarkable adventures during his extraordinary ninety-five years, but some of the fondest memories I have of him are from my childhood, walking hand-in-hand with him in Piedras Negras, a Mexican border town just across the Rio Grande from Eagle Pass. Everyone, and I mean everyone, in Piedras Negras—in the marketplaces, bars, and little cafés—knew him. And he knew them, too.

Big R was a straight-up, six-foot-five, strikingly handsome man. But when he met somebody on the street, he would bend right over and hug them. He hugged them all: men, women, children. And they would hug him right back, especially the women, and especially the older ones. He would say in Spanish, "Meet my son, Royito," and the hugging would start all over again with me. Especially the women and especially the older ones.

By the time I was old enough to walk, I was old enough to hug. And hug I did.

He taught me early on to say hello to everyone. To wave to everyone. To tell people you love them and mean it. To give flowers, or fresh-shelled pecans, or pears, or Krispy Kreme doughnuts. To share everything you have with others. He was a man who never met a stranger, and because of him, I never have either. His lesson was one of compassion, drawn

Be kind to everyone you meet, because everyone is fighting some kind of battle.

from the wisdom of the Scottish theologian John Watson: Be kind to everyone you meet, because everyone is fighting some kind of battle.

But the thing Big R taught me that I cherish the most is that as a man, it is cool to hug everyone. As a dad, he never, ever hesitated to give me a public hug. And while I may have been a tad embarrassed by it a few times in my life, when I was a kid, that was just the way it was.

I have applied his lessons—especially to hug—the best way I know how in my life of family, friends, faith, and work. I hug Mary, my wife of more than thirty-five years; my kids, Courtney, Ashley, and Shay; friends; and other family members to excess. I also hug my business partners and employees. And I hug CEOs, presidents of the United States, receptionists, football players and coaches, secretaries of state, and four-star generals. I even tried to hug the Queen of England once in the Texas Governor's mansion when Ann Richards was governor. That did not go well. But it didn't stop me from hugging senators, governors, folks on the street, musicians, employees, and taxi drivers. It's just the way I was brought up. Anyone worth meeting is worth hugging.

❖ ❖ ❖

One night, I had a vision that spurred me to a new understanding of the power of the hug.

It was four weeks after my dad passed away. I was in Frankfurt, Germany, with two colleagues, David and Jay, on an important business trip. We took the overnighter from the States and got to Frankfurt early on a Sunday morning. I couldn't sleep on the plane. It happens. But to avoid horrible jet lag, we had to make ourselves stay up until at least seven o'clock that night by walking and talking, seeing the sights, walking and talking, sharing a meal or two, walking and talking. Finally, we were beat; our eyes were so heavy from lack of sleep that we stumbled back to the hotel and quickly bid each other goodnight.

I called Mary and then hit the sack, ready to get hours of sleep, which is rare for me. As I shut my eyes, all alone in a strange hotel bed, it hit me. Since the memorial service for my dad, I had *buried* myself in family and work. Now here I was, sleep deprived, far away from home and family. It began to rain—and rain hard—outside. Trains were running right outside my window with their hollow rhythm. I was thunderstruck, and I began to shake—not from fear, but from the brutal truth. It was vividly clear: I was a sixty-year-old kid with no parents. I am all alone, I thought.

I had never needed a hug more in my entire life.

And so it came. Gently at first, I felt a hug deep in my heart. My dad and mom were hugging me. I was certain of it. I wasn't seeing them, but I was feeling them. It was not a memory: I could feel them, just as I had felt Mary hug me before I left for the airport. It lasted for a marvelous while, soothing my mind and giving massive comfort to my body and soul. But then a very strange thing happened. As the hugs started to slip away, my eyes popped open, and I was wide awake and energized. I looked at the clock and was astounded—it was only 8:00 p.m. I felt like I had slept through the night. But it had only been an hour or so!

That's when the vision for this book came to me. Nobody had physically touched me, but I had been healed nonetheless. *I've gotta start writing about the power of hugs*, I thought. So I wrote the title of a little book of hugs—*The 10 Essential Hugs of Life.*

As the rain, trains, and clock measured the span of the night, I began to imagine the story of the ten hugs. As morning came and I was still wide awake, now going on forty hours with a sixteen-hour day ahead of me, I walked down to the business center and typed out the titles of the book chapters. By the time I was done, it was time to meet David and Jay. I immediately told them about the book. Both of them yawned and patted me on the back, and David responded with these words of inspired encouragement: "We're late to our meeting." At that precise moment, I knew I had an idea worth pursuing, even if they didn't at the time.

I believed in the power of the book because I believe in the power of a hug. I believe that each of us can lift people up, heal some hurts, and spread a little love. I carry many things in my messy wallet (got that habit from my dad, too), but among them I always keep several quotes taped to the inside pockets. One of my favorites is from *The Shack* by William Paul Young:

> If anything matters everything matters. Because you are important, everything you do is important. Every time you forgive, the universe changes; every time you reach out and touch a heart or a life, the world changes; with every kindness and service, seen or unseen, my purposes are accomplished and nothing will be the same again.

Doing little things to touch a heart or a life changes the world forever. Healing ourselves and others heals the world. Shining a light on goodness spreads good in the world. Sharing love with another breeds love around the world. Writing this book was emotional and powerful for me, but I did not write it for me. I wrote it for you. I wrote it because I hope to change your life for the better, even if only a bit.

"I love hugging. I wish
I was an octopus,
so I could hug ten
people at a time."

—Drew Barrymore

THE PURPOSE
OF HUGS

As a wise person once wrote,
hugs are the universal medicine.

When you go on a journey of hugs, you find so much richness in the language they represent. A hug says, without a word, that you are special and important, that I've been thinking about or worried about or missing you, and that everything—if just for a moment—is okay in the world.

I have heard and read many maxims about the power of a simple hug, maxims like "A hug is a handshake from the heart" or "a bandage to a wound" or "the shortest distance between friends." All true.

But I think the most compelling purpose of a hug is that it is the universal symbol that we are all pretty much the same: No matter our title or status in life, we all need to be loved and cared about. A hug is the great equalizer. As Denver Moore said in the gripping book *Same Kind of Different as Me*, "The truth about it is, whether we is rich or poor or somethin in between, this earth ain't no final restin place. So in a way, we is all homeless—just workin our way toward home."

I decided several years ago to walk across America: to go on the road with a backpack, a couple of small American flags, a camera, and a mission to take a picture of something good in every mile I traveled. I've made it through seven states so far.

It was the second day of my walk, and I had already covered some twenty miles when I found myself in Warren, New Hampshire. I was beyond exhausted, and as I was trying to find a place to stay in town, I saw an older woman with shining white hair. She was standing all alone on the side of the road. Should I walk on by or stop to say hello? Well, you know me. I walked across the street, introduced myself, and asked, "Are you okay?"

She smiled a little and said, "Yes. I just took a little walk, and my house is right over there. Would you like some tea?" I really wanted a beer, but I said, "Of course." We walked hand in hand and went into her small New England home, where she fixed me some hot tea. It took a while, but as she made the tea she told me about herself. Her name was Dot. She had been married for more than fifty years, and her husband had just passed away. And she had never left the county that she was born in. Not once. Some might think that because she was unworldly, she might also be unwise. But I proved that false with one question.

She had been a junior high school teacher for over forty years. That inspired me to ask a question that has always intrigued me, but that I never got to ask my own schoolteacher mother. I told her about Mom, and then I said, "I have always wondered about those kids who are a real problem as teenagers. What is the ingredient that makes a troubled kid grow into a good adult rather than a bad adult?"

Dot's hands shook as she took another tiny sip of her tea, and then she looked me in the eye and said, "I don't know for sure. But here is what I saw in those forty years. The troubled young kids that ended up being good people and good parents had someone in their lives—a mom or dad, or maybe an aunt, uncle, grandparent, a parent of a friend, a coach, a teacher—some adult who told them, 'I love you and I am proud of you,' and who gave them a hug."

I love you. I am proud of you. A hug. We all have times when we are troubled. We all need these things, and not only when we are troubled.

The 10 Essential Hugs of Life is for all of you out there who are looking for just a little help getting on with it, help with reaching out and connecting with someone you love, help with discovering and expressing appreciation for the goodness in life, help lifting your spirits and the spirits of those around you. Maybe there is somebody you miss and want to reconnect with. Maybe you've found yourself stuck in your journey on the road of life, trying to sort some things out or discover some healing and inspiration. Now, I am not any kind of health or mental health professional. If something traumatic has happened in your life (and I pray that it hasn't), you and possibly a medical expert know better than I do how to help you heal. But I believe in the raw power of living through loving and hugging, and that's a good first step for any situation. I hope *The 10 Essential Hugs of Life* hugs your heart.

If you decide to read this little book of hugs, you can thank Big R, the ultimate man hugger. And a shout out to the men out there–hug everyone, but hug your fathers and sons a lot. Even if it doesn't seem manly. There are not many bigger men than Big R, and because he hugged me and told me he loved me all the time, I knew that he did. There are a lot of people out there who don't know, who are crying out for someone to love them and hug them, who are wishing that they could love themselves a bit more. And when they feel more love, it will change their lives, and it will change the world. So don't waste any more time.

Hug on!

"Hug, but don't linger."

— Colleen Barrett, retired president of Southwest Airlines

THE WAYS TO HUG

Some of the most important hugs
don't involve touching at all.

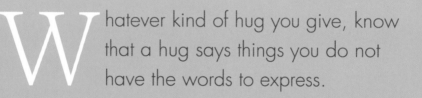

Whatever kind of hug you give, know that a hug says things you do not have the words to express.

Do not throw hugs away just because you are not a natural hugger. I come from a family of huggers, so it is natural for me. Some people come from a family of musicians, and so music is natural. Or sports. Or cooking. Or farming. But if you don't come from a family of huggers, it doesn't mean you can't become good at hugging. Hugging, like anything else, it takes practice and patience. And it helps to understand the purpose of hugs and the different ways you can give them. If you believe in the healing and uplifting power of hugs and don't know how to start, let me give you the basics. If you don't feel comfortable hugging total strangers, that is just fine. Some hugs—some of the most important hugs—don't involve touching at all.

THE MIND HUG

A big step in dumping the garbage

Years ago, a friend broke my heart. Our friendship has never been healed. I was hurt too badly to mend fences.

The hurts and fears and anxieties we experience in life can be a heavy burden. As time goes on, each one is added to the pile of garbage we carry around, pushing us down. I was certainly carrying that burden. But one day, I simply reached my limit. I'm not sure I knew exactly what I was doing, but I began to think back on the times my once-friend and I had enjoyed together. It occurred to me that one of the best days of my life was a day I had spent with him. I recalled the person he was on that day, and in my mind, I hugged that person. I couldn't hug the person he had become, but I could hug the person he once was to me. It was an authentic hug. "I wish you well," I thought, and I meant it.

That Mind Hug liberated me from the burden of hurt and anger. It allowed me to let go.

Ann Richards, the much-beloved 45th governor of Texas, used to grab me by the cheeks and say, "Precious, get over it and get on with it." The Mind Hug is that first big step toward doing both. It helps you safely engage with the hurt or anger or anxiety you carry around every day. When something deep inside is pushing you and nudging you—when you need to dump some of the garbage, as my preacher, Gerald Mann, says—take that first step of self-healing.

If you've been hurt, think back to a moment when you loved the person who hurt you. Hug her and say, "I wish you well," and mean it.

If you are feeling anger or anxiety or self-doubt, face it. Recognize that with the help of our beautiful imaginations, we can indeed make mountains out of molehills. Some of our fears and anxieties are deep—so deep we can't see them. When they

Get over it and
get on with it.

do rise up, embrace them with the mind, not the heart—say, "I see you"—and sooner or later, they will become less scary, less powerful. Give them a Mind Hug and free yourself.

If you continue to ignore that pile of garbage, it will keep growing. Stop avoiding it, piece by piece, and then find a way to let go. No one except you and your God will ever know you took that first step. The embrace happens in the privacy of your mind, which makes it the most powerful hug. We can't change anything until we change our minds.

The Mind Hug is a rational hug, not an emotional one.

After a Mind Hug, if it feels comfortable or natural, you might reach out and try to mend fences, or you might move on to the more emotional hugs. But even if you don't, at least you have addressed the pain or doubt or anger with a hug, not with hate or negativity. So whatever it is that's weighing on your mind, reach out with a Mind Hug and see what happens. It won't hurt. It might help. And it's free.

THE HEART HUG

A Heart Hug gives the good in your life a heartbeat.

Yes, we all carry around negative garbage, but we also carry memories of special people and moments in our lives, memories that bring an unexpected smile or a twinkle to the eye.

And grabbing hold of those wonderful memories is just as important as letting go of the negative.

This is easier said than done. The world today is so much about what's wrong and horrible and what divides us as humans. It seems harder and harder to carve out any room for happy things. That's where the Heart Hug comes in.

Every day, all day, we have memories of good things—people and events—that flash through our minds and make us happy. The most common memories usually aren't of the big moments, but of the small ones spent with the people and in the places we love the most. Most of us let them go right by and focus on what's making us sad or frustrated or disappointed. Don't do that anymore. Instead, Heart Hug those moments of goodness. Grab onto them with all your heart and hug them tight. Then say thank you.

Heart Hug the precious moments of your past.

Thank you, Granddaddy, for showing me how to garden and how to name the daylilies and roses after people I love. Thank you, Momma, for the most important lesson of my life: Don't waste any of your precious life trying to be average at what you are bad at; instead, life live to the fullest by spending your time and talent becoming great at what you are good at. Thank you, sister Mary Gordon, for always reminding me that there is magic in the mundane. Thank you, Bill Blagg, for lesson number

Grab onto the moments of goodness with all your heart and hug them tight.

thirty-three: Whenever you get down or depressed, just throw all your problems in a pile with everyone else's, and you will take yours back. Thank you, Peter Romig, for always reminding me to love the life I was dealt. Thank you, Uncle Gordon, for taking me on a trip to Washington and showing me a bit more of the world. Thank you, Papa Joe Couri, for teaching me to drive as slow as I want to in ice and snow, no matter if the people behind me are honking—a lesson that recently saved my life. Thank you, Sittee Martha Couri, for showing unconditional kindness to everyone you met. Most of all thank you, sister Susan, the most amazing person I have ever known, for teaching me that you don't have to have legs to fly. These are hugs of love and emotional connection. Hugs of thanks.

Why do we let those memories slip by and slip away? Many of them force your heart to ache a bit. Remembering your granddad who isn't with you anymore. Remembering a pet you lost. Remembering a friend you haven't seen in a long while. Remembering your lost youth. We shut these memories down so as not to feel nostalgic or sad or alone. Don't shut them down. Heart Hug those sweet, loving, and, yes, even sad moments, and you will feel closer to those you love and those you have lost. You will find that the embrace of the Heart Hug will give you peace of mind, as well as pure moments of inexplicable happiness.

Heart Hug the precious moments of your present.

Just as we have precious memories of the goodness in our past, we have precious thoughts of the good events and people in our present. Hold on to them, cherish them, and be thankful. When you wonder what your children are doing right this moment, pause and give them a huge Heart Hug for all of the joy they've brought to your life. When you know your spouse or partner is having a tough day, pause and give him or her a Heart Hug for being your partner and for standing by you through thick and thin. When your thoughts go out to friends who are serving our nation, Heart Hug their courage and their commitment to making the lives of others better. Hold these people and moments close, because they are shining beacons of goodness in our daily lives.

Be thankful for the goodness in life, whether it's past or present. I am convinced that when you really Heart Hug someone, their heart feels the hug whether that person is in the next room, the next house, the next country, or the next life. And it does your own heart good to give a Heart Hug. In fact, I am convinced that Heart Hugs do wonders for the heart of the world.

Try a Heart Hug once a day. It will become a heartfelt and loving habit.

THE TOUCH HUG

Every time you reach out to touch a heart or a life, a life changes.

As I have wandered through life on the road to understanding and fulfilling my purpose, whether I'm in schools or at the State Department, in diners or boardrooms, in grand hotels or grocery stores, at the White House or the House of Pancakes, I have noticed that when I reach out and touch someone, they are changed, even if it's only for a moment. Whether it's a hand on the shoulder, a genuine handshake, an authentic smile, a "How are you?" or a "Thank you so much" or a "Great job," or even a hearty wave, there are few things more healing and caring than a natural, authentic Touch Hug. (And there's nothing worse than a fake one.) When you change someone's life for the better–again if only for a moment–yours is changed too. This is the power of the simple and genuine Touch Hug.

Today, people everywhere are starving for affection—including you, by the way. Everyone keeps their head down, focused on their new "protective armor": smartphones. These and other hand-held devices are the perfect tools for cutting you off from any human contact.

So here is a moment of truth. Just put that protective armor in your pocket or purse and wander around a schoolyard. Talk

When you change someone's life for the better, yours is changed, too.

to the people raking the leaves, give them a pat on the back, and say *thank you* for keeping the school clean for the kids. Mean it. When you are in the checkout line, say thank you to the cashier or the person sacking (that's what we call bagging in Texas). The next time you're in a reception area waiting for your meeting, instead of just saying "Good morning" or "How are you" to the receptionist, reach out, shake their hand, and say, "Thank you so much for helping me," and mean it. It will blow their mind and expand your heart. If you are a natural hugger, help them feel even better with a hug.

Every single time I stand in an airport security line, whether it's a short line or one that zigzags right out of the airport, when I give the TSA representative my driver's license and they look up to make sure I am who I say I am, I look back at them and say, "As a frequent flyer, I really appreciate what you do." And I mean it. And as I'm walking away, once they've moved beyond stunned silence, I hear a heartfelt "Thank you" right back.

I use the Touch Hug all the time, whether I'm working with Fortune 500 companies or mom and pops. I can't tell you how many people have said, "Thank you. You have no idea how much I needed that."

You don't have to actually touch someone to really touch them.

Put your cell phone down. Log off of your computer. Remove your iPod headphones. Reach out and Touch Hug people everywhere you go. It might just be the easiest hug of all—and with it, the world changes.

THE BEAR HUG

The mother of all the hugs—the loving hug

Big R had little use for any hug but the Bear Hug.

Every morning, Dad would go down to the bank to drink free coffee with the other old men in town. And most afternoons, he'd head down to Palace Drug to drink free coffee with the local coaches and other towns folk. Dad never paid for coffee. And when he walked into either place, he would make every single person get up and give him a Bear Hug. "I'm not gonna let you get by with just shaking my hand," he would say. And he hugged those people every chance he got, until he just couldn't anymore.

The Bear Hug is the miracle hug because it bundles all of the hugs, Heart, Mind, and Touch, along with love, into a healing wonder moment. It can be as gentle as your baby's first tiny hand-hold or the fierce hug of long lost brothers or sisters. The Bear Hug does not depend on physical strength, but rather the genuine and authentic strength of the love that

The Bear Hug does not depend on physical strength, but rather the genuine and authentic strength of love.

comes through in that hug. My dad loved every person in our town, and he wasn't afraid to show it. They in turn loved him and hugged him back. Then they hugged me, too.

Bear Hug those who need it the most. Incredible congratulations after graduation. A long lost soul mate. A lost pet that was found. A daughter who just had one of her own. A son who had one of his own. A brother who just got back from war. A sister who was shaken to the core. A business partner who made the sale—or who lost it. A teacher who taught so well. A father who just retired or a mother who was just hired. A lifelong friend who is about to go. A brand-new friend who is out in the cold.

Bear Hugs are necessary in a life lived to the fullest, and they're the most special when there is nothing to celebrate at all—when they are simply about love that is shared with someone close.

Mind. Heart. Touch. Bear. Hug on!

THE 10 ESSENTIAL
HUGS OF LIFE

Hug # 1

HUG YOURSELF FIRST

When you hug yourself,
it frees you to hug others.

"Don't forget to love yourself."

—Søren Kierkegaard

So many of us are taught at an early age to "love your neighbor as yourself." I try to live according to that principle. But in order to love your neighbor as yourself, you have to love yourself first. Loving yourself—not worshipping yourself—is the only way you can love others. So first, hug yourself.

My older sister, Susan Spence, was born in 1945. She was a beautiful baby, but she had spina bifida, a congenital birth defect caused by the incomplete closing of the neural tube inside the spine. The nerves that were supposed to run down her spine and into her legs instead burst through the bottom of her spinal cord. Susan was never supposed to have left the hospital alive. But my mother and my granddaddy, Gordon Griffin, had other ideas, and they eventually brought Susan home. Because of my mother and the rest of our family, Susan graduated from high school and junior college, had her own apartment, and lived to be forty-nine years old.

When Susan passed away, I was sleeping on the floor of her apartment. When I woke up and found sister Susan still, I had a moment of truth so powerful that it rocked my very soul. For almost forty years, my mom and dad, my sister Mary Gordon, and I had all helped Susan get around in her wheelchair. For those forty years, I thought I had been pushing Susan. Suddenly I realized that she had been pushing me.

Susan, with all of her outward obstacles and her massive list of I-never-got-tos, would sometimes get so down. But then she would look at me and say, "I like me. I like who I am." Susan was giving herself a Heart Hug. If she could do it, you can do it.

Right now, wrap your arms around your body, give yourself

a big ol' Bear Hug, and say, "I love you and I miss you." I love you. And I miss you. The seven most healing words anyone can say to another person. So why not say it to yourself? I bet you really need it. We all have times in our lives when we wish we could just get away from ourselves, when we've headed down a dark road and feel there's no light to be found, when we can't remember what there ever was to love. Instead of focusing on or trying to escape from the parts of you that you may not like right now, hold on and reclaim the things that you love and miss about yourself.

What is it that you miss about yourself? Reflect deeply on the times when you were happy and content with yourself, when you were feeling good about yourself. Give that "you" a Heart Hug. Personally, a few years ago, I began to ache—you know that sad ache that you can't quite explain. Eventually I realized that I ached because I missed the old Roy, the Roy who didn't take himself so seriously, the moments of raw joy that I used to give out easily and freely, the easy smile that I always had for friends and family, the giddy love of life. So I gave the old Roy a hug. Now I do it all the time, and when I do, two things happen:

1. I smile for no reason.
2. I can breathe.

What is it that
you miss about
yourself?

If you repeatedly hug yourself—the self you like best—it becomes a positive addiction. You have the power to change your own life. So reflect on what you miss the most about yourself, write it down, and go hug it to life.

My mother used to say, "Roy, whenever you start believing your own BS or are feeling bad about yourself, you've got to break the cycle and hug who you really are. Don't try to be somebody you are not. You are who you are—so hug the real you." So often we let our view of ourselves and of the world get clouded by things beyond our control. Or we let other people influence who we are trying to be. We become a lesser version of somebody else. Instead, focus on being a better version of yourself. Be the best that you are.

A few years ago, I found myself facing a unique day. I was born on October 10, and so in 2010, my birthday would be 10-10-10. As the day approached, I admit that I got a bit super-stitious and took a look at my horoscope for the year, which I *do not ever* do. *What the hell*, I thought. And even though I never read horoscopes, the last line of this one resonated with me, and I remember it to this day (and probably will to the end of my days): "Your best bet in the next year will be to recognize your own inherent value—not just what you appear to be worth to others."

For me to become a better me or for you to become a better

J.H.

John Henry Won

you, we must first begin to understand our inherent value, the value that is our authentic hearts and souls. Once you realize that you are important—and that you matter—you'll have begun to assemble a better you.

When you hug your best self, you are refusing to give up on the goodness inside of you. What is the heart of that goodness? Nine times out of ten, you are happiest—you are feeling that goodness—when you find yourself by getting lost in the service of others. Gandhi was certainly right about that. And so hugging the best of you lights up the darkness in this world almost instantly.

I was once told this parable and have since seen the truth of it in other forms. While many debate its origin as an actual Native American story, it deeply reflects what I believe about our ability to be our best selves.

An old tribal elder was teaching his grandson about life. "A battle is going on inside me," he said to the boy. "It is a terrible fight between two wolves. One is anger, envy, greed, arrogance, self-pity, resentment. The other is joy, peace, love, humility, kindness, generosity, compassion. The same fight is going on inside you, and inside every other person, too."

The grandson considered this for a moment and then asked his grandfather, "Which wolf will win?"

The elder replied, "The one you feed."

When you hug yourself, you feed the Good Wolf.

If you don't hug yourself first, there's no way in the world you can hug everybody else. If you aren't celebrating the best of yourself, you can't bring out the best in anyone else. Life is not a dress rehearsal, as they say, so hug yourself first and give the best of yourself a rebirth.

Hug #2

HUG YOUR FAITH

Your faith grows stronger knowing you have faith.

"All I have seen teaches me to trust the Creator for all I have not seen."

— *Ralph Waldo Emerson*

When you reach higher ground, you will find that fences are mended, barns are raised, disputes are resolved, and solutions are created—all for the purpose of serving the greater good. Have faith in goodness. For God is good.

My dad, Big R, always referred to God as the "Great One." Every Sunday morning before church he would cook an awesome Tex-Mex breakfast for us. He was famous for his refried beans with cheese and white onions and his hot sauce made with incredibly hot chili pequin peppers. They were staples in the breakfast at the Spence household every Sunday. Before we could sneak even one bite, though, Dad would read us a story from the lesson that would be taught at the adult Sunday school. We were starving, but he went on and on, unfazed. And at the end of the lesson, he would say, "We give thanks in the name of the Great One."

Dad would hug his faith at the Sunday morning breakfast table with all of us.

Decades later, when I was writing *The Amazing Faith of Texas*, my colleagues and I discovered that one simple concept seemed to unite all the faiths of the world: the Golden Rule. Why is that? Because the Golden Rule is a reflection of goodness in the world and within us, and that is what we all ultimately believe in, regardless of what church or temple we walk into every week. Faith in goodness is what unites us.

Despite news to the contrary, we believe that the Golden Rule rules—for every faith has a version of it as part of its foundation:

"In everything, do to others what you would have them do to you; for this is the law and the prophets." —Jesus, Matthew 7:12

"What is hateful to you, do not do to your neighbor. This is the whole Torah; all the rest is commentary." —Hillel, Talmud, Shabbat 31a

"Not one of you truly believes until you wish for others what you wish for yourself."
—Muhammad, al-Nawawi Hadith 13

"Treat not others in ways that you yourself would find hurtful." —the Buddha, Udanavarga 5.18

"One word which sums up the basis of all good conduct . . . loving-kindness. Do not do to others what you do not want done to yourself."
—Confucius, Analects 15.23

When you hug your faith—the heart of what you believe— you are hugging goodness, you are hugging the Great Oneness. When you grab hold of your belief in goodness and refuse to let it go, you will see it in the world, and you will make it happen in the world. I find that when I try to hug the Golden Rule, when I am treating people (both friends and strangers) as I would like to be treated, I feel better about myself and the world. And in turn, it seems the world feels a little better about me, too.

Faith in
goodness is
what unites us.

As I mentioned before, I am walking across America to discover and to help bring to life the goodness of our people and our amazing spirit. And on this journey to find good, I found the road to higher ground. What I learned is that we become what we look for. Look for good, and you will become good. Hug your faith, practice your faith, practice goodness, seek goodness in the world, and you will be a force of good in the world.

I'll fess up for my mother and tell you that she wasn't particularly religious, but she sure understood goodness. And for her, anything that was good and decent was God. She used to say, "Evil is easier. Being mean to people is easier. Hate is easier. Gossip is easier. Running away from responsibility is easier. But it will pay off if you embrace goodness in all that you do." It will pay off because it will carry you along the long road to higher ground, where goodness rules. On higher ground, good is the single driving principle, anchored in the higher purpose of improving all lives. Finding higher ground is a long journey, but it is worth the walk.

When you are standing on higher ground, there is no getting around your faith, your belief. You feel the force of good in the world, see the goodness that exists in everything. For you, that may mean seeing God in everything. Higher ground is a place of clarity. You develop a keen, rich sense of the

Everybody's Welcome

events and people in your life, seeing them as they are, not as you want them to be. And because of that, you will hold yourself accountable for the decisions you make; you will see the right and just choices. They won't all be easy. But they will be good. And they will set you free.

If you look for hope, it will lead you to higher ground.

Robert Frost was right—there are two roads in the wood:

Road no. 1. If you look for enemies, you will find them. If you look for hate, it will bring you down and break your heart. If you seek gossip, it will consume you. If you look for fear, it will follow you all your life.

Road no. 2. If you look for friends, you will be befriended. If you look for love, it will live in your heart and lift you up. If you seek the truth, it will set you free. If you look for hope, it will lead you to higher ground.

Whichever road you choose will define your life. Don't be afraid to hug what you believe in. We are no better than when we are being true to our values, when we are doing good in the world and seeing good in the world. So hug your faith, because if you don't, you will drift away from this road, and you may not like where you end up.

Hug your faith close, rise up to higher ground where goodness rules, and once you're there, pull others up to stand next to you.

Hug the Great One. Hug goodness. Hug your faith.

Hug #3

HUG YOUR FAMILY

Yes, all of them.

"Smile at each other, smile at your wife, smile at your husband, smile at your children, smile at each other—it doesn't matter who it is—and that will help you to grow up in greater love for each other."

—*Mother Teresa*

Family members—
hate 'em or hug 'em.
I say go for the hug.

When my dad died, I received so many notes sharing personal stories of relationships between fathers and their children. Most were from people I knew, but not all. Some were from people I thought I knew well, but I've come to find out that everyone has an untold story. They all seemed to need to share. Maybe they felt comfortable telling me their stories because they could see that I had been blessed with an amazing sixty-year run with my dad.

The stories fell into four buckets.

The rare. Some told me how lucky they felt to have had a relationship like the one I had with my dad—long, loving, hugging, fun. But these were few and far between.

The young. So many stories came from people who knew or learned about my dad and who were moved to share because they had missed out. These were touching stories about how young they were when their dad passed away. Five years old. Seven years old. Nine years old. Nineteen years old. And so it went, story after story. These people wanted to tell me how lucky I was and that they always think about what might have been if their dad could have been with them as they grew up and had a family of their own. It was heartfelt, and I simply listened and then hugged them—Heart, Touch, or Bear.

The hard. Many told me stories of the falling out that they'd had with their dad, the anger and the pain, but finally, in the end, the reconciliation. There was a sense of remorse but also a greater message: "I am so grateful that we made our peace."

The painful. Some told me stories about the falling out that was never patched up, the forever pain. If this has happened to you, start right now with a Mind Hug and then proceed to a Heart Hug if you can. It is never too late.

A family is what it is. Whether you like them or loathe them or love them, you can't get away from yours. Why fight it? A big family or a single mom, an adopted parent or even a coach or teacher, we all have people who've touched our lives and influenced who we are today. We should touch their lives, too. Of course, every family and each family member is different. But there is a fabric that binds them together. As much as you might try to cut that fabric, every time you cut it you are actually cutting yourself. You do not have to like them all; you simply have to hug them all—easy hugs, not-so-easy hugs, even no-way hugs.

The easy family hugs. When most of us were little, we hugged everything. Even stuff we weren't supposed to hug. We hugged moms and dads, brothers and sisters, neighbors,

You do not have to like them all; you simply have to hug them all.

Family Tree

cousins, aunts, uncles, other little ones, and anyone who would reach out. We hugged stuffed animals, real animals, pillows and blankets, even poison ivy. When we are little, hugging is easy. We aren't carrying all the garbage we collect as we grow up. When we become moms and dads, aunts and uncles, grandmas and grandpas, we become huggers again with any little thing that crawls, walks, laughs, or cries its way into our arms. It is so natural and vital when you have little ones.

Sometimes, the easy family hugs stay with us. Every time we see a dad or a brother or a cousin, we get that same sense of joy, and we have no choice but to share it with a big Bear Hug. We all need people in our lives to share an easy family hug with. They are the most joyful.

The not-so-easy family hugs. It seems as if at one time or another, every family has a prodigal son or daughter, mother or dad, uncle or aunt or cousin who leaves the fold. You know the ones. One of them might be you. Either they keep the bridge intact but seldom come back, or they simply blow up the bridge completely. And what happens is the hug version of the Cold War. Most of the time, the parties involved in the family Cold War don't actually seek to hurt one another, but they do. I believe that reconciliation with family is so important to a life well lived. One person breaking down even one stone of the wall, even with only a Mind Hug to let go of the pain, can begin and complete that journey.

The no-way family hugs. "And I mean it—no way." "She is the most selfish and hurtful human being." "It will be a cold day in hell before you see me hugging him." Maybe you have

"Happiness is having a large, loving, caring, close-knit family in another city."

–George Burns

someone in your family that you say similar things about, maybe not. If you do, here is a tip.

I was at a Land Rover driving academy years ago. The driving instructors were insane. They had driven Land Rovers over the most wicked terrain in the world, and they believed these machines could do anything. They had no fear, and they wanted you to have no fear, too.

The instructors were also in a real sense Zen masters.

I was driving when David, my instructor, told me to slow down and go to the very edge of a straight-down cliff. I did. We stopped and kept the engine running.

David said, "We are going to let this machine ease off the cliff into the unknown. And here is the blinding truth. If you put your foot on the brakes even a tap—this vehicle will flip over and we will probably die. On the other hand, if you just ease on the gas—just a tiny tap on the gas—and let the vehicle go on its own, we will be just fine."

I said, "Are you insane? I am not going off this cliff—I can't even see the bottom."

David looked at me kindly, and almost whispering, he said, "Roy, sometimes you just have to let go."

I stared back, tapped the gas, and we went flying into the unknown—down the side of the cliff into a huge mud and water hole. And when the machine came to a stop, covered in so much mud we could not see out the window, David repeated his wisdom: "Sometimes you just have to let go."

Consider a Mind Hug for that "no way" family member. Let go of the pain and the hurt, wish them well, and then get on with it.

Every family has a story. Some are loving stories of family members who hug each other and say, "I love you." For those of you from loving families, let me tell you how lucky you are and encourage you to hug your family even harder. Some are sad stories of families who almost never hug. For those who have had the toughest lives, who feel they never had that family hug, let me say that God hugs everyone.

Regardless of your own family's history of hugs, you can always partake, as my good friend Scott Perkins said, in the Global Hug. In my lifetime there have been many momentous events—sometimes painful and sometimes glorious—that have brought together the big family of humankind, even the no-ways, onto higher ground for a Global Hug. The assassination of President John F. Kennedy, the first step on the moon, the fall of the Berlin Wall, the space shuttle *Challenger* disaster, 9–11: In these moments, the human spirit rises to lift all of us up, and that Global Hug is felt around the world.

But day to day, what most of us need to live a rich life are family hugs.

Your family is your family. The ones you love, Bear Hug the stink out of them. The ones you like, give them a good ol' Touch Hug. If there's bitterness with some, you can Mind Hug them. The easy hugs, the not-so-easy hugs, even the no-way hugs. Just hug your family.

Hug #4

HUG YOUR FRIENDS

Many times they need it and
don't even know it.

"The only way to have a friend is to be one."

—*Ralph Waldo Emerson*

E verybody wants to be a friend but many don't want to deal with the "ship." But friendship—in good times and bad— is the stuff of a life well spent. So hug your friends—just because

- They might be fighting a battle and really need it, whether you know it or not. They need your love.

- They are special to you, and everyone needs to be important to somebody.

- It will bring you closer, it will make you feel better, and it will make them feel better. You have the power to touch their lives.

You can choose your friends. You can have as many or as few as you want. And you can make new friends out of strangers with a hug. This makes hugging friends one of the most important things you can do to improve the quality of your life—and the quality of theirs. Old friends, new friends, potential friends—hug them all.

Hug your old friends. More than forty years ago, I met my friends and business partners for life at the University of Texas at Austin. (Hook 'em Horns!) We started a company called Media '70 while still in school, and when we graduated, we decided to launch a marketing and advertising agency. We had three goals:

1. Stay together.
2. Stay in Austin.
3. Make a difference.

Today, we are

1. Still together.
2. Still in Austin.
3. Still trying to make a difference.

Partner*ship*. Relation*ship*. Friend*ship*. What we began so long ago has weathered good times and bad, highs and lows, because we did whatever it took to keep the "ship" together.

Our ship has gone through many changes. As we all grow older, we all grow differently. That's life. But we also grew stronger. And while the partnership and friendship are not the same as when we started (nothing ever is), we lived our dream together and are finishing it together as lifelong friends. Pretty rare—pretty special. I, for one, am so thankful. Hug your old friends, and the friend*ship* will keep sailing.

I hug my friends all the time—Heart Hugs, Touch Hugs, Bear Hugs.

Hug your new friends. As you wander through life, you make new friends. Victor Borge, comedian and pianist, once said, "A smile is the shortest distance between two people." I believe the shortest distance between new friends is a smile and a hug. And unlike your old friends, your new friends are more of a mystery to you. You simply don't know as much about them. To get them to let their guard down, try letting your guard down. You will find that the act of hugging speeds up the process of building a lasting friendship. Hugging is the great accelerator of closeness.

Hug your lost friends. Losing a soul mate brings on sadness. What we miss most about our lifelong friends is the life they brought to ours. The best way to lighten our sadness

"Wishing to be
friends is
quick work,
but friendship
is a slow
ripening fruit."
–Aristotle

The Goat

is to make time for a Heart Hug. Think of times when you were together, a moment you shared that makes you smile or laugh. Heart Hug it, and that moment will be forever embedded in your heart. That's the joy of Heart Hugs.

If you've lost a friend because one or both of you chose to abandon the ship, it can be difficult to climb aboard again. If you simply need to get over it and get on with it, give that person a Mind Hug. But if you can think of one moment of

Hugging is the great accelerator of closeness.

pure friendship between you that makes the pain or hurt or anger begin to lessen, Heart Hug that lost friend. Maybe your heart will take the lead, and you will find yourself reaching out and reconnecting, making the next step to a Touch Hug. Just remember what an unknown poet once wrote: "A simple friend thinks the friendship over when you have an argument. A real friend knows that it's not a friendship until after you've had a fight."

President Lyndon Johnson used to say, "Vote early and often." I say, "Hug early and often." Everyone is fighting some kind of battle, even if you don't know it. And your friends need and deserve your support.

Hug your friends. Your old ones. Your new ones. Your lost ones. Because friends are what make the world go round.

Hug #5

HUG YOUR FLAG

All of us come from somewhere
and have, at the least, someone.

"I had rather be on my farm than be emperor of the world."

—*George Washington*

Hugging your flag isn't simply about being patriotic; it is about being thankful for the goodness in your community.

Not many people hold ties anymore to the place where they grew up or to the places that influenced who they are now. Most of us move away because moving away is easier than it used to be, and we're more exposed to the wider world. That physical distance creates other distance—distance from culture, from beliefs, from people and communities that once made a difference, from our roots. Some of us want this distance. Reinvention seems to be the theme of the twenty-first century.

No matter how far you travel, though, you cannot run away from where you came from. It isn't everything that you are, but it is a part of who you are, and you've got to hug it. Hug it to celebrate or heal.

If you came from a safe, caring, nurturing, wholesome, loving place, you need to be grateful for the goodness in your life and hug that place. I've already shared with you the importance of hugging your family—yes, all of them—and you might have a lot of reasons to do so. But also go back and give that special teacher a Bear Hug. Think back to special moments growing up and give your community a Heart Hug. Hug those special memories, hug the crossing guard, hug the things that made the place that you are from special. Be honest and acknowledge that you were blessed. And then give the greatest hug, the greatest form of gratitude, and find a way to pass that blessing on. You owe it to yourself and to humanity to spread that goodness.

Now, maybe your life has been very different. We are all fighting some battle. Sadly, some people—and I may be talking to you—start fighting those battles when they are young because they come from a dangerous and scary place. Bad homes. Bad neighborhoods. Bad friends. Bad childhood experiences. Some of them really bad. But if you are reading this now, you probably aren't there anymore, and there is a reason. Maybe that reason is a community that rallied to protect you. Maybe it is a teacher who saw potential and offered encouragement. Maybe it was one person who offered a hug when you needed it most.

Find a shining, wonderful memory of one good thing. A special place. A special friend. A special church. A small story that brings a smile and a happy ending. A person or event that had a profound, positive impact on your life. Hug it with your heart and be grateful. Give the good its rightful attention. Because the light is just as much a part of where you came from as any of the darkness.

Me? Every day, I'm thankful that I grew up in Brownwood, in Texas, in America. Ours was a classic small town from inside a Norman Rockwell painting. Palace Drug, Dairy Maid, Friday night football, Main Street, a loving family. Our town

Acknowledge
that you were
blessed . . . and
find a way to pass
that blessing on.

Hayden, Texas

and my life weren't without their moments of darkness, but I was blessed, and I know it. I was particularly blessed to be born in a country that was born to be free, and I hug that all the time. My mother was a civics and American history teacher, and thus my family was highly opinionated and political. We talked and debated politics more than any other topic by far. And as I grew up, I realized that no matter how rough or heated or frustrating the debate is here in America, politics is the business of freedom, of life, liberty, and the pursuit of happiness. So I hug my country every day and thank God for my freedom.

You can't run away from where you came from, so dump the garbage, find the goodness, and hug it. Hug your flag.

Hug #6

HUG YOUR FAILURES

You can own them or they can own you.

*"Character cannot be developed in ease and quiet.
Only through experiences of trial and suffering
can the soul be strengthened, vision cleared,
ambition inspired, and success achieved."*

— *Helen Keller*

There is a huge difference between failing and coming up short. Coming up short is simply playing all out and not winning. Failing is a violation of character. Don't confuse the two.

Those who know me know that I am a fierce competitor. Around the office, I used to wear a T-shirt that said, "Second place is first place for losers."

Years ago, the advertising agency I founded with my friends had an opportunity to do a new business pitch for a company that was shopping for an agency. I happened to know the chairman of the company, and he got me a lunch with the president. Well, that probably wasn't the best move, as it turned out. At the lunch, the internal politics of the company became clear. The president told me, although not quite so directly, that he, not the chairman, was the decision maker, and because of my relationship with the chairman, there was no way my company was going to get the business.

I knew we were destined to lose.

Let me describe what agencies go through when trying to win new business. They spend hundreds of thousands of dollars, and employees spend countless nights and weekends away from their loved ones to prepare just one pitch, to try with all their might to win one new account. Pushing the pitch forward would clearly be a huge waste of resources and a drain on our staff. The right thing would be to pull back.

Back then, every time we lost a pitch, I felt it was my failure. So as soon as I heard that we wouldn't win, I wanted to win all the more. Now I had something to prove. Instead of sharing what I knew with my team, I pretended that I hadn't heard anything of the kind. We pushed forward, and sure enough, after much sacrifice and cost, we lost.

For many years I was consumed with the idea that failing was not winning. What I know now is that the lost pitch was not a failure. We came up short. When playing the game of life, you're going to have bad days, and you're going to come up short. You're going to make mistakes. You're going to be late, bomb an interview, forget a birthday, lose a game. Coming up short is being late to pick your son up at the library. Failing is not caring if you're on time or not.

So the lost pitch was not a failure. And yet, *I had truly failed*. My number-one job as a purpose-based leader is to protect the troops. Instead, I sent the troops into a heart-wrenching, destined-to-lose battle out of false pride and bravado. I led them into certain defeat. Wanting to win isn't wrong, but I made a decision that hurt people and an organization that I had helped build and that I cared so much about. When I made that decision, I knew in my heart and soul that it was plain wrong. Yet somehow, in my mind, I justified it. That was my failure. That was flawed judgment.

I was haunted for a long time by that failure. I tried to ignore it, but I felt it weighing me down. It took time for me to realize that hiding from a failure doesn't make it go away. Instead,

Stay Together

Fess up when
you mess up.

I had to do as my friend and preacher, Dr. Gerald Mann, instructed: Fess up when you mess up. And when you do, you will begin the process of reclaiming your future.

Mind Hug your failures—fess up, move on, and try with all your might to live a life in which you don't have to fess up anymore. Try to live the truth. If you don't hug your failures, they'll haunt you and will cast a sea of darkness on your future.

Real failures can be hard to hug, I know. Any self-help guru will tell you that to get over it and get on with it, you have to forgive yourself. Most of us try to do that, but we leap to the forgiveness, jumping right over the all-important step of fessing up. None of us want to admit that we have knowingly hurt or betrayed another person, that we made a terrible mistake. We avoid fessing up because we believe that if we shine a light on our failures, we'll never be able to forgive ourselves. And so those failures keep lurking in the shadows, haunting the edges of our psyches. In fact, you will never be able to forgive yourself *until* you fess up—to yourself and, sometimes, to others. You have to shine a light on those dark moments if you're going to help goodness shine through.

The things we do matter. Pretending that they don't matter won't change that fact. Fessing up allows us to get over it and get on with it, and it keeps us from messing up all over again—at least in the same way. Owning your failures is the only way to halt the cycle of rinse and repeat bad behavior.

Hug your failures. And give your future a chance to shine again.

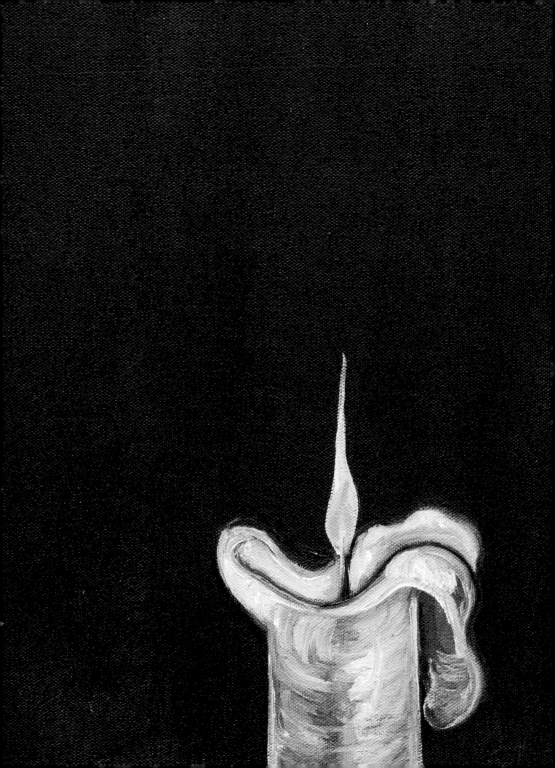

Hug #7

HUG YOUR FEARS

Fears have fears, too.

*"Everything will be okay in the end;
if it's not okay, it's not the end."*

— *Anonymous*

Fear loves the darkness. It fears being exposed. It would much rather haunt and bully you from the shadows of your mind, heart, and soul. Hug your fears, shine a light on them, and bring light to the darkness.

Some fears are real. Some are simply illusions. My wife, Mary, creates an awesome haunted house full of illusions every year on Halloween. Kids love it. Adults are more trepid. As we grow, we put more stock in false fears—those outside and in. They help us run from the real. Instead, dump the illusions, and hug the real fears that may be limiting you.

When I was a safety and quarterback on our high school football team, I used to get so nervous before the game that I would actually throw up. After a good gargle of Listerine, I was good to go. Now, there are a lot of other football players who've admitted to doing this, but when I was in high school, I didn't know about them. *Football players don't throw up*, I thought. I was so embarrassed that I would do everything in my power to hide it. I was terrified of somebody finding out.

About midseason in 1967, one of the assistant coaches came up to me and said, "Roy, have you thrown up yet?"

I was devastated. "Yes, sir," I replied with my head low.

"Good! I'll keep this our little secret." I was humiliated, but at least only one person knew.

We had an amazing season, and right before the final state championship game, the legendary coach Gordon Wood approached me as we prepared to take the field against Bridge City.

"Roy, have you done it yet?" he asked.

"What? Done what?"

"You know . . . thrown up!"

Oh no, I thought, *Coach Wood knows*.

With eyes cast down I said, "No, sir, Coach. For some reason I feel just great today. I don't know why, but I'm not going to throw up. "

"Well, son, if you don't want to blow the whole season and disappoint your teammates, coaches, school, and the whole town, get in there and get it done."

It worked. I was so scared I ran into the bathroom, *got it done*, gargled with Listerine, and hit the field. That day we won the Texas high school football state championship, winning 14–0 to cap off a perfect 14–0 season.

My fear of people finding out that I was throwing up was a paralyzing fear. But it also wasn't the real fear, the reason I was throwing up in the first place. As I thought about Coach Wood's words that day, I realized that my true fear was letting people down, myself included. And to this day, I still have that fear. But now I hug it!

Whenever I talk to people about hugging our fears, they noticeably pull back. I get it. Most of us would rather run from our fears; facing them isn't easy. But your fears love the darkness. Hug them; shine a light on them. They probably won't

See the Light

If we don't hug our fears, if we don't embrace them as a part of who we are, they will haunt us.

go away, but you might navigate your way around them in the clear light of day; in the darkness you never will.

How do you hug them? How do you shine a light onto them? Don't believe that if you ignore them they will somehow go away. Identify what the real fear is. Ask yourself, "Why am I afraid of that?" Get past the surface, the symptom, to discover the deeper fear. Get it out. Say it out loud. And then Mind Hug it. Say, "You might try to take me down, but I'm not giving up without a fight."

I know that my deep fear is letting somebody down. I don't throw up anymore, but I still feel that fear. I feel it when I'm getting ready to give a speech. I still want to give the speech, so I practice more. I feel it when I'm leading a great team of people. I still want to lead those people, so I work on learning how to be a better leader. I do whatever it is I need to do to maneuver around that fear and keep moving forward.

We all hold deep fears in our hearts and minds. The fear of losing a precious loved one. The fear of losing your job and your security. The fear of losing your home or some other critical support. The fear of letting your family, your friends, yourself down. Real fears. But if we don't hug our fears, if we don't embrace them as part of who we are, they will limit us.

Here is a secret: Every fear has the heart of a coward. Fears seem to have the heart of a warrior when they lurk in the shadows. But when you expose them—when you Mind Hug them, face them, shine a light on them—their true colors are exposed and they scurry away.

And then you are free.

Hug #8

HUG YOUR FUTURE

Never, never give up on your dream.

*"Do not go where the path may lead; go instead
where there is no path and leave a trail."*

— *Ralph Waldo Emerson*

If you can dream it,
you can build it.

In 1998, President William Jefferson Clinton, who I am lucky enough to call a friend, visited South Africa. While there, Nelson Mandela took him on a tour of Robben Island, where the South African president was held for eighteen of the twenty-seven years the he had spent as a political prisoner. Bill told me about that visit just as he wrote about it in his 2004 autobiography, *My Life*. As the two men stood in the tiny cell and looked out at the quarry where Mandela had toiled, they had an emotional and powerful conversation. Bill asked his wise friend, "I know you did a great thing in inviting your jailers to your inauguration, but didn't you really hate those who imprisoned you?"

Mandela replied:

> Of course I did, for many years. They took the best years of my life. They abused me physically and mentally. I didn't get to see my children grow up. Then one day when I was working in the quarry, hammering the rocks, I realized that they had already taken everything from me except my mind and my heart. Those they could not take without my permission. I decided not to give them away. (*My Life*, 782–3)

Your future is your heart and mind; it is your passion; it is what you love to do; it is your *dream*. Most importantly, it is your purpose in life. You have to Mind, Heart, and even Touch Hug your future, hug it tighter than anything else. If you don't, you may give it away without even realizing it.

People (myself included) get all tangled up and get frenetic about living for tomorrow, about doing what we are supposed to do. Yes, we all have responsibilities, but if we aren't careful, we come to believe that we can't fulfill our responsibilities at the same time as we follow our dreams and achieve our purpose. But the only way that the world can take away your future, take away your dreams, is if you choose to let those things go. You have to refuse to give up on your dreams. Hug your future, every moment of every day. Today, perhaps more than ever in modern history, we need to inspire and enable people from all walks of life to follow their passion and purpose. To take that first step right now and begin to live their dreams.

If you want to take that first step in discovering your purpose, write down what you *love* to do. Don't think about what you *want* to do or what you are *supposed* to do. For example, I love to make hot sauce. The inspiration came from my dad. So now my family and I make and sell Royito's Hot Sauce, sharing the love of my father's hot sauce and values. And on the back of every jar we print our purpose: "To inspire people to Don't Do Mild in life by following their purpose and passion."

The only way the world can take away your future, take away your dreams, is if you choose to let those things go.

The Road

What do you love to do? Cook? Invent? Write? Teach yoga? Create films? Build haunted houses? Work with your hands? Sing? Fish? Teach? Preach? Build? Defend people? Garden? Play the piano? Help older folks? Save pets? Knit? Make holiday cards? Take pictures? Fix stuff? Run? Ride? Really, what do you *love* to do? Whatever it is, hug it. Go do it now. And then find a way to do it as much as possible. I promise that

"Where talents and the needs of the world cross, therein lies your vocation."

–Aristotle

if you dream big, if you are willing to pay the price in terms of hard work, and if you show grit and optimism throughout, you can make a living and a life doing what you love to do.

If you do what you love, you will never have a job. You will simply have work to do. Work that you love, that you master, and that therefore improves other people's lives and your life, too. You will burn out trying to be average at what you're bad at. You'll never burn out trying to be great at what you're good at. Doing work that you love is how you hold on to your heart and your mind, how you hold on to your future.

No matter how tough the going gets, hope for your future will lead you to higher ground. Hug your future so tight that it is impossible *not* to take that first step of what may be a one thousand mile journey, the greatest journey of your life.

Your fantasies. Your hopes. Your passions. Your purpose. Hug them hard and often. Because doing what you love to do is the stuff that dreams are made of.

Hug #9

HUG YOUR FIRSTS

And keep doing new stuff everyday

"Twenty years from now you will be more disappointed by the things that you didn't do than by the ones you did do. So throw off the bowlines. Sail away from the safe harbor. Catch the trade winds in your sails. Explore. Dream. Discover."

— Mark Twain

Instead of making New Year's resolutions that are mostly punitive, make a new bucket list every year—new things to explore and try. Trust me, you are more likely to actually do new and exciting things than accomplish a list of don'ts.

Do you remember your first day of school? I sure do. Vividly. I had impetigo and ringworm at the same time. I had to walk into school with red iodine on my head and yellow sulfur on my arms (those were the unfortunately obvious treatments in the fifties). I had to sit in the back of the room, away from the other kids, and when they all went outside for recess, I had to stay inside by myself.

My teacher took pity on me and gave me some M&Ms. By day three of this situation, though, I had just about had enough. When she was out of the room, I went into her closet, found the big bag of M&Ms, and ate every last one. And then I was horribly sick. To this day, I have never eaten another M&M.

That was a whole lot of firsts in just a few days—and I remember them vividly not because it was horrible, but because it was thrilling. Walking into school the first time, braving the other kids' stares, sneaking into the teacher's closet. All of it was exhilarating. And when I think back and give those days a big Heart Hug, it inspires me. I want to feel that excitement again.

Heart Hug the firsts in your past. They will make you smile, laugh, cry. Your first day of school. The first teacher you loved. Your first bicycle ride past the end of your driveway—the freedom you felt. The first girl or boy you were smitten with, the first kiss—the excitement you felt. The first touchdown, piano recital, solo—the pride you felt. The first time you drove alone, the first date in your own car, the first out-of-town road trip with your buddies. The first concert. The first year at college. The first job. The first boss. The first paycheck. The first apartment. The first beer bought legally. The first time you actually fell in love, real love. The first home. The first time you held your baby, and the next. And then *their* first days of school. And on and on.

Do whatever is necessary to hug your firsts. If you ever have trouble remembering, play the music of your youth. It will take you to places you think you have forgotten. No matter your generation, in our society, music is the timeless memory trigger. Visit your old haunts. See old friends. Because even when hugging your old firsts brings sweet sadness—and sometimes it will—the memories of the nervousness, the buzz, the joy, will push you to try new firsts.

My dear friend Jim Collins says that you're only as young as the new things you do—the number of firsts in your days and weeks. And I believe that. When you're a kid, every day is full of firsts, full of new experiences. As you get older, your firsts become fewer and fewer. If you want to stay young, you have to work to keep trying new things. You have to choose never to retire from life.

If you can't remember the last time you felt the thrill of trying something new, you're in a rut.

Free at Last

If you can't remember the last time you felt the thrill of trying something new, you're in a rut. If you feel bored, you're in
a rut. It's time to go hug a first. Take a new route home. Try a
new restaurant. Paint a wall in your house purple. Jump out of
an airplane. Say to yourself, "I wonder what the world has in
store for me today. I think I'll go find out." Do something that

makes today memorable. Do something that makes you love life again.

Hug your firsts. Hug your old firsts to make you smile and make you want to feel the excitement of new firsts. Hug new firsts to keep you young and always moving onward.

Hug #10

HUG YOUR FINALS

Hug your finals and new doors will open.

*"What appears to be the end may really
be a new beginning."*

— Unknown

Until my dad passed away, I did not know that when one really hugs a final moment, that hug opens up a world of brand-new firsts.

Some finals in life are splendid: the final day of school, the final day of work before a long vacation, the final payment on a car. These finals we hug because they are liberating, uplifting, joyous. But some finals in life are humbling, sad, even devastating. These finals we hug so that we can be liberated, so that we can get over it and get on with it.

"When one door of happiness closes, another opens; but often we look so long at the closed door that we do not see the one which has been opened for us." Helen Keller said this. She could not see, yet she was always searching for the next open door. She understood that finals are a part of this thing called life, and as we grow, we experience more and more finals. You can run from them. Or run to them. You can try to forget them, or you can hug them with your mind and your heart. If you choose not to hug your finals, you will waste your days standing in front of a closed door, waiting for it to open again. And you will miss all of the firsts that final created. Because every first begins with a final.

Instead, choose to hug a final and recognize that the door is shut, that it won't open again. When you look up, you'll see a new door standing open.

I started writing this book because of a final. I was all alone in Germany hugging my final moments with my parents, my final understanding that I no longer had them with

Every first begins
with a final.

me. Hugging those finals helped me understand how to honor them and helped me head toward a new first.

What final in your life is waiting to be hugged? Have you hugged the last day you spent with your mom or dad? Have you hugged the final day your son or daughter spent in your house before heading off to their adult life? Have you hugged the final moment you loved a significant other before recognizing that the relationship wouldn't last? If you feel that you are being held back in life, there is likely a final in your past that you need to recognize, hug, and move past. Finals are inevitable.

My wife, Mary, and I and our family enjoyed to the fullest twelve fun and loving years with our black Labrador, Ellie, whom my son picked out when he was a boy and Ellie was just born. Ellie was perfect. No, really, she was. We called her Gandhi. She was an emotional and loving part of our entire Spence tribe and all who entered our home and hearts. After twelve active years, she developed a very weak heart, and in the end we had to make the gut-wrenching decision that so many of you have had to or will have to make.

With Ellie in our arms, with my wife and daughter whispering words of love, and with me sobbing, resting my head gently on her, and hugging her, I whispered, "Thank you." I was thanking her for giving all she had to us unconditionally

for all the days of her life. When her last breath came, all of us (absolutely true) felt her heart rise up and fly out into the next wonderful world.

The moment after Ellie's death tested me deeply on the idea of hugging your finals. I didn't want to. I wanted to run from this emotional loss and pain. And then, as I was pacing and wiping the tears off, knowing now for the first time that I would never again be with Ellie physically, it came to me, just as it had come to me when I first had the idea for this book of hugs. Ellie was hugging me; her big brown eyes stared straight into mine. I Heart Hugged her so tightly, realizing that beyond food and water, that was all she had ever needed from me. People who love their pets and who at some moment have to part from them know exactly what this story is all about. Hugging your finals liberates you from pain—not all of it, but the worst of it, the piercing part of it.

As long as you are living, the only door that never closes is the door to your future. The more finals you hug, the more firsts you will capture in their wake. And the more life you'll live. So hug all of your finals and turn them into firsts.

HUG ON!

J uan Mann returned home to Sydney, Australia, with a world of trouble on his shoulders and no one to greet him, to hug him, when he arrived. As he watched fellow travelers smile and walk into the open arms of loved ones, he felt a longing.

So he took action. With a piece of cardboard, he made a simple sign: free hugs. He found a busy intersection, held up the sign, and waited. His first taker was a woman whose dog had just died and whose daughter had died one year before. From there, a movement was born: The Free Hugs Campaign.

Around the world, people began holding their own Free Hugs signs or wearing Free Hugs T-shirts.

Free Hugs went viral—the original video on YouTube has more than 73 million views. Why? Because all of us naturally understand the power of a hug.

The 10 Essential Hugs of Life are interconnected circles of healing and happiness. Each one is important, and you can't create a joyful life without all of them. Use the power you hold in your mind, heart, and arms to lift spirits, including your own. Use the Mind Hug, the Heart Hug, the Touch Hug, and the Bear Hug to build bridges, offer genuine love and empathy, and move beyond obstacles. Hug your way out of the dark and into bright goodness. Hug your way to higher ground. Be like Big R: Be kinder than necessary.

A huge Heart Hug for my wife, Mary Spence, and for the entire Spence family.

And hug on!

ACKNOWLEDGMENTS

Huge Hugs

To my mom, Ruth Spence, and my dad, Roy "Big R" Spence, for hugging me and always telling me they loved me and were proud of me. For all the Spence Tribe hugs, especially my sisters Susan and Mary Gordon. To my wife and partner, Mary Couri Spence, for always supporting me and covering my back on my many times frenetic journey of dreaming and building and for reminding me that "affecting individual lives is more powerful than I sometimes give it credit." To my awesome kids whom I adore, daughters Courtney and her husband Tom and our joyful grandchild Madison—a.k.a. Sunshine, and Ashley and her husband Jason and my son Shay for always saying to me about my new adventures, "Go for it Dad!" To my business friends and associates and partners in this dream of The 10 Essential Hugs of Life, Judy Trabulsi and Karen Greer Bearden for pushing and improving and encouraging; David Crawford for always being the most amazing design talent in the world; Liz Hamel for the HUGS calligraphy; and especially my creative partner and Illustrator Jared Dunten for his inspiration and his passion for bringing to life The 10 essential Hugs of Life. To my most excellent editor Lari Bishop, the Greenleaf Publishing Team and their awesome designer Neil Gonzalez and my Smith Publicity Team for loving and championing the power of hugs.

Also a huge hug to all the people out there who encouraged me to keep on.

I encourage everyone to Hug on!

ABOUT THE AUTHOR

ROY SPENCE

Roy grew up in Brownwood, Texas (population 19,000), and his childhood was full of love, security, and yes, hugs. He came from a family of huggers—especially his dad, Roy Sr.—and early on he realized the power of hugs. He attended his beloved University of Texas at Austin, and in 1971 Roy and his three partners started GSD&M, a highly successful advertising and marketing firm headquartered in Austin, Texas. Under Roy's leadership, his agency has helped grow some of the world's most successful brands, including "Don't Mess with Texas,"

Southwest Airlines, Wal-Mart, DreamWorks, the PGA TOUR, BMW, the US Air Force, L.L.Bean, and the Clinton Foundation.

Roy Spence is author or coauthor of three books, including the bestseller *It's Not What You Sell, It's What You Stand For* and *The Amazing Faith of Texas*.

Today, Roy is cofounder and CEO of The Purpose Institute as well as chairman of the board at GSD&M, and he leads major companies all over the world to help them discover their purpose. He is a strong advocate for inspiring young people to go out there and make a living and a life doing what they love to do, believing that entrepreneurship is the Miracle of America. He speaks throughout the country on the power of purpose in one's life.

ABOUT THE ILLUSTRATOR

JARED DUNTEN

It seems fitting that the Rio Grande is where I broke my neck and became paralyzed during a diving accident. "Rio Grande" is Spanish for "big river," and that moment was and always will be a big part of who I am. That time of my life was a lot like that river. Shallow in some places, deep in others, with lots of twists and turns.

I started working at GSD&M around 1998. I enjoyed my work and loved the people I was working with. When Roy approached me about working with him on his book and creating the paintings for each of the ten hugs, I agreed before he was able to finish explaining the idea. I knew it was a special project and wanted to be a part of it.

In 2004 I was awarded a student membership to the MFPA (Mouth and Foot Painting Artists), based in Lichtenstein.

I married the love of my life, and we live just outside of Austin. Kimberly and I have two beautiful boys, and life just keeps getting better. I continue with physical therapy and look forward to the day when I can run around Town Lake again. I will paint myself out of this wheelchair.